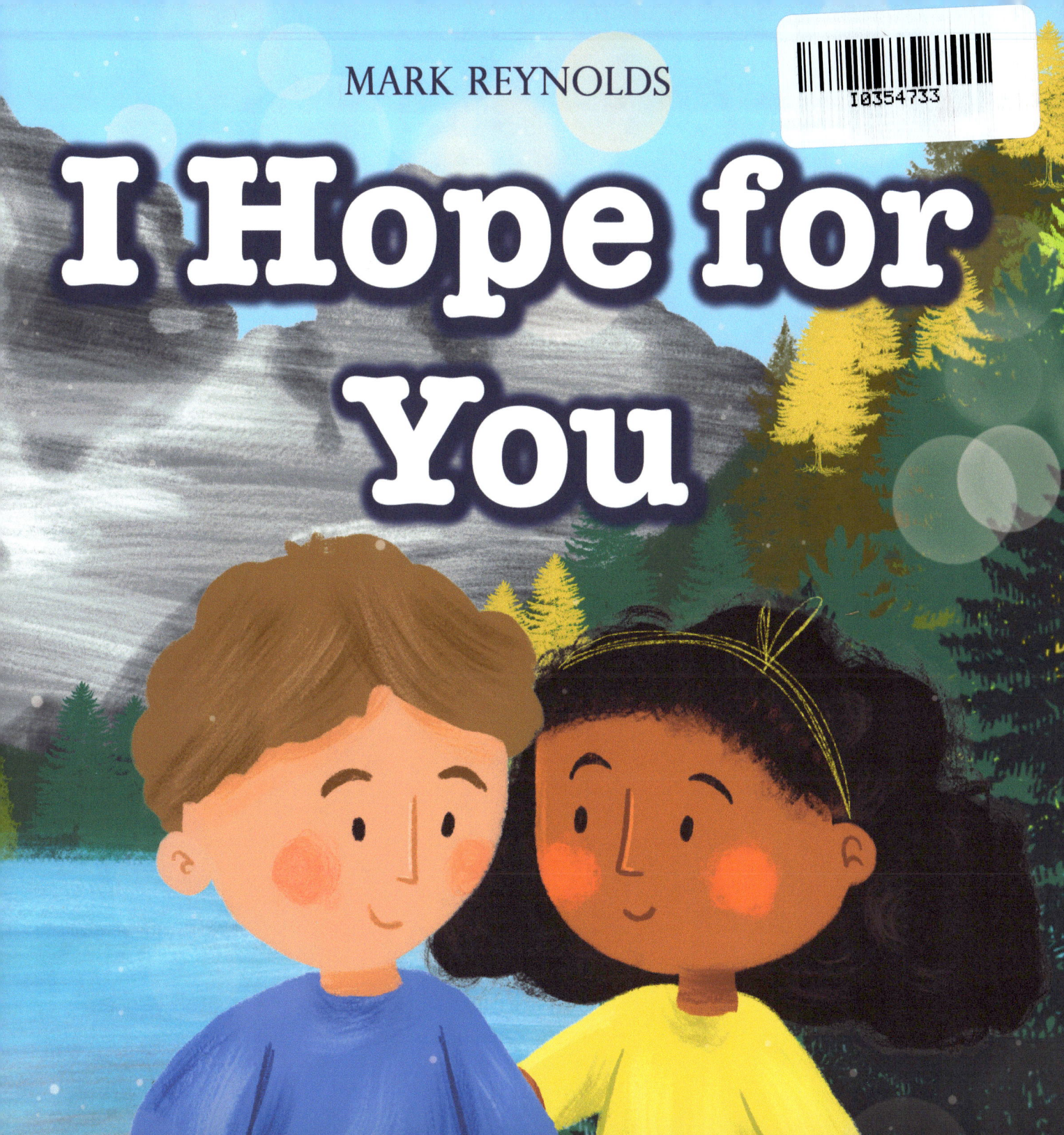

Copyright © 2021 Mark Reynolds. All rights reserved.
No part of this book may be reproduced in any form without permission in writing from the publisher. Printed and bound in the USA.

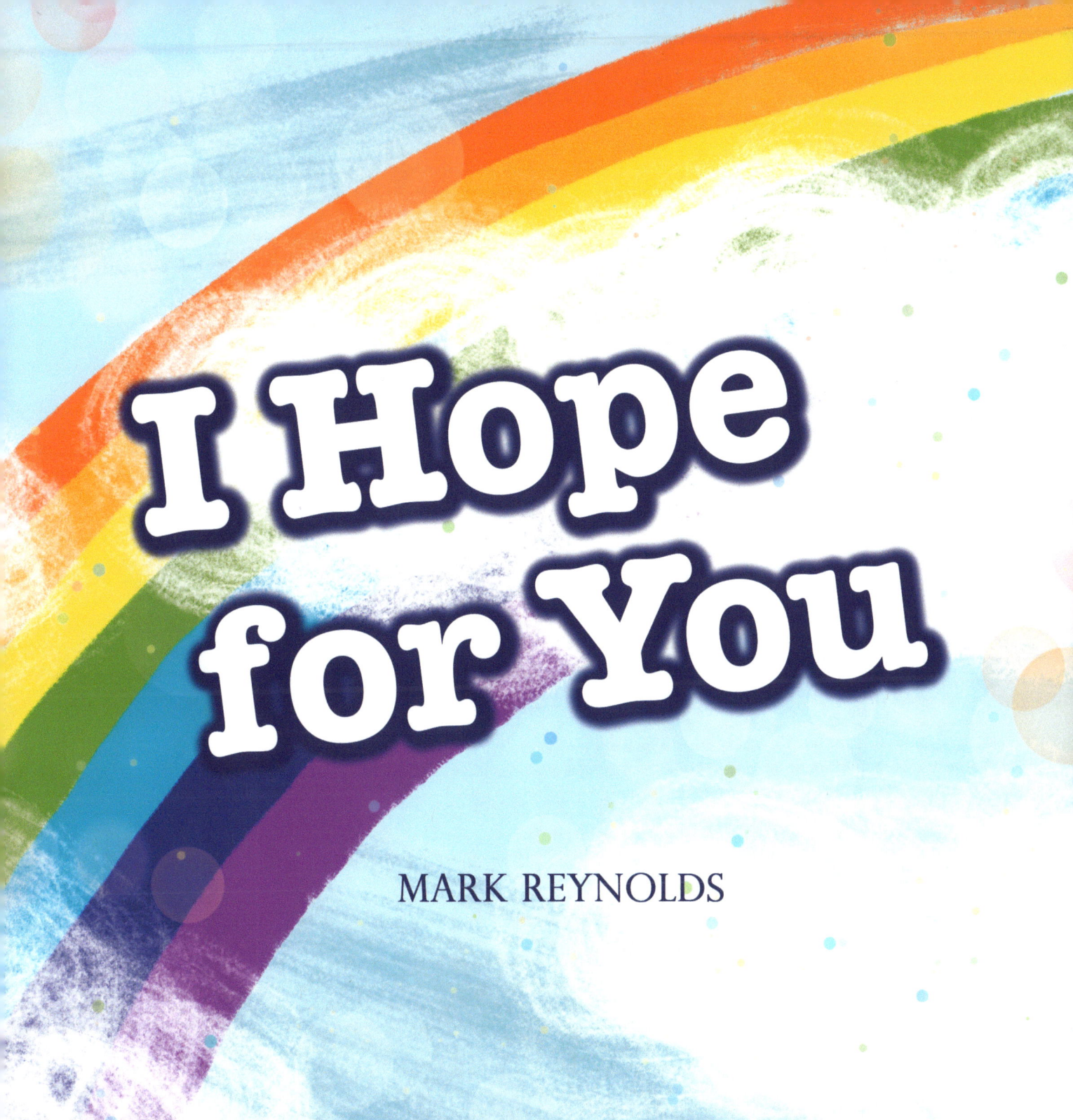

I hope for you **joy** in everything you do,
That **happiness** finds a way to you.

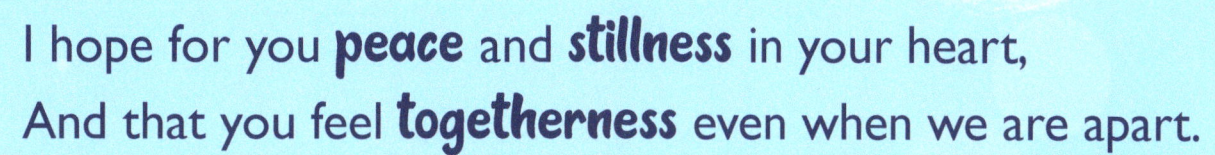

I hope for you **peace** and **stillness** in your heart,
And that you feel **togetherness** even when we are apart.

I hope for you **laughter**, that you see the humor in everything,
Even when events happen and failures sting.

I hope for you **bravery**, that you can conquer all your fears,
That you always follow through with things, even if you have to fight back tears.

I hope for you **security**, that you always feel safe and sound,
That even when you feel like you're dangling, you can still place your feet on the ground.

I hope for you **peace** when chaos surrounds you,
That **calmness** finds its way and prevents you from feeling blue.

I hope for you a **grateful heart** in every single way,
That you remember to count your blessings each and every day.

I hope for you **confidence** when there seems no other way,
The **courage** to speak up and stand up for others each and every day.

I hope for you **creativity**, that you are inspired to create and make,
That your art continues to improve with each new step you take.

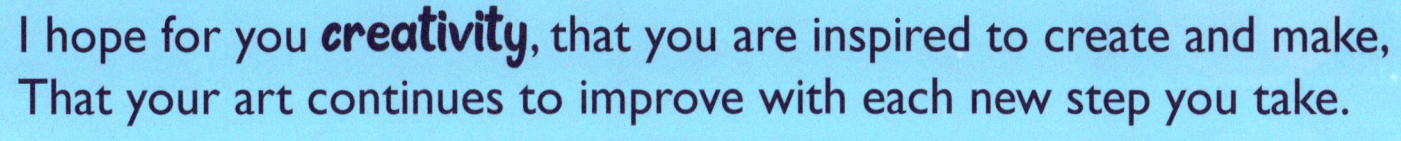

I hope for you **happiness**, that you are more happy than sad.
The key to happiness is finding the good in the bad.

But of all the things I hope for you, there is nothing else above
My deepest wish and want for you: *I hope for you **love***.

www.ingramcontent.com/pod-product-compliance
Lightning Source LLC
Chambersburg PA
CBHW041524070526
44585CB00002B/74